EXPLORERS DISCOVERING THE WORLD

THE EXPLORATION OF

NORTH AMERICA

Tim Cooke

Gareth Stevens
Publishing

Please visit our website, www.garethstevens.com. For a free color catalog of all our high-quality books, call toll-free 1-800-542-2595 or fax 1-877-542-2596.

Library of Congress Cataloging-in-Publication Data

Cooke, Tim.
 The exploration of North America / Tim Cooke.
     p. cm. — (Explorers discovering the world)
 Includes index.
 ISBN 978-1-4339-8624-6 (pbk.)
 ISBN 978-1-4339-8625-3 (6-pack)
 ISBN 978-1-4339-8623-9 (library binding)
 1. North America—Discovery and exploration—Juvenile literature. 2. Explorers—North America—History—Juvenile literature. I. Title.
 E45.C66 2013
 970.01—dc23

                              2012021921

Published in 2013 by
Gareth Stevens Publishing
111 East 14th Street, Suite 349
New York, NY 10003

© 2013 Brown Bear Books Ltd

For Brown Bear Books Ltd:
Editorial Director: Lindsey Lowe
Managing Editor: Tim Cooke
Children's Publisher: Anne O'Daly
Art Director: Jeni Child
Designer: Lynne Lennon
Picture Manager: Sophie Mortimer

Picture Credits
Front Cover: Library of Congress: inset: **Thinkstock:** istockphoto main.

All photographs, prints and drawings **Library of Congress** except, **Clipart:** 23b; **istockphoto:** 18, 33; **Public Domain:** 20r, Chris McKenna 24; **Robert Hunt Library:** 37; **Shutterstock:** 5b, 36, John Brueske 22, Dave Allen Photography 5t, A&N Protasov 39, Eric Von Seggern 3, Deng Songpuan 29, Kenneth Sponsler 35, Wild Arctic Pictures 27b; **Thinkstock:** Comstock 11, Hemera 14, istockphoto 7t, 45, Photos.com 16, 19, 30-31; **Topfoto:** Fotomas 44, The Granger Collection 12, 31b.

Brown Bear Books has made every attempt to contact the copyright holders. If anyone has any information please contact smortimer@windmillbooks.co.uk

Manufactured in the United States of America
1 2 3 4 5 6 7 8 9 12 11 10

CPSIA compliance information: Batch #CW13GS. For further information contact Gareth Stevens, New York, New York at 1-800-542-2595.

CONTENTS

INTRODUCTION

No one knows who were the first explorers of North America. By the time Europeans arrived at the end of the 15th century, the continent was already home to many different groups of native peoples. But Europeans largely treated North America as a "New World" that they could exploit.

Throughout the 16th and 17th centuries, European pioneers made the dangerous voyage across the Atlantic Ocean. They were drawn by stories of gold, beaver fur, and fertile land for settlement. They discovered a continent of vastly varied landscapes.

Dividing the Continent

Spanish explorers focused on the Southwest and the West Coast. French trappers explored the wild and icy far north, in what is now Canada. British settlers settled on the East Coast. It was not until the 18th century that frontiersmen led the way across the continent. They sought a route from the East to the West Coast that would bring the United States together.

The Blue Ridge Mountains largely stopped British settlers moving inland until they were crossed in the mid-17th century.

The first Europeans to see the Grand Canyon in Arizona were soldiers from the expedition led by Francisco de Coronado in 1540.

CHRISTOPHER COLUMBUS

Christopher Columbus is probably the most famous explorer of all. He was an Italian who worked for the rulers of Spain. He sailed the Atlantic to look for a new sea route to Asia. When he found land, he thought he was in the Indies. In fact, he had reached a "New World": America.

This painting shows Columbus claiming the "New World" for Spain and offering a prayer of thanks for his discovery.

Clouds hang low over a rain forest on a Caribbean island. Columbus mistook the fertile islands for the Spice Islands of the Indies, in Asia.

A direct route to the Indies would bring a chance to make huge profits from spices. From old books he had read, Columbus believed wrongly that the Earth was about half its real size. He thought he could find a route to the Indies by sailing west.

Setting Out

Columbus persuaded King Ferdinand and Queen Isabella of Spain to pay for a voyage. On September 6, 1492, he left the Canary Islands with three ships. By October 10, the crew members were so unhappy they threatened to only sail for three more days. But two days later, they saw land.

DID YOU KNOW?

Columbus's three ships were named the *Santa Maria*, *Pinta*, and *Niña*. The ships carried a total of 87 crew members.

HI-TECH SHIPS

Columbus's ships were caravels, the most advanced vessel of the time. The caravel had been developed by the Portuguese just for exploration. It was small and nippy. Its shallow keel meant it could sail up rivers. It had triangular, or lateen, sails. They made it possible to sail into the wind. But there was very little space on board, so the crew was always uncomfortable.

This painting shows Columbus greeting local people. He hoped that they might eventually lead him to riches, such as sources of gold or silver.

Columbus named the land San Salvador. Local people showed him a way through the Bahamas to Cuba. Columbus believed that he was in China. But when he sent sailors to look for the capital city, they found a village of huts.

Return to Europe

Columbus founded a colony on the island of Hispaniola then sailed home. He arrived in March 1493. News of the new route to "Asia" spread. A few people guessed that this was not Asia, however, but a "New World."

DID YOU KNOW?

In 1498, Columbus sailed along the north coast of South America. He said he had found the Garden of Eden from the Bible.

Three More Trips

Columbus returned to the Americas three more times between 1493 and 1504. He visited the coast of Central America. But his efforts to found a colony failed. The Spanish rulers once had him arrested for governing it badly. Worse still, he could not find gold or spices, or even a way to Asia. Ferdinand and Isabella lost interest in his voyages. It seemed that his trips had come to nothing.

DEATH OF COLUMBUS

Columbus died in May 1506, 18 months after his fourth voyage. In his opinion, Ferdinand and Isabella had never fully rewarded him for his achievement. He had lost control of his colony on Hispaniola. He had not found any treasure or the sea route he still believed led to Asia. Columbus was disappointed with his career. But today we know he was an outstanding sailor who changed the face of the known world.

Columbus lost very few men to shipwreck or disease. He had the ability to get his crew to follow him, even when they were unhappy or scared.

9

1513–1520

JUAN PONCE DE LEÓN

Juan Ponce de León was a Spaniard who had sailed with Christopher Columbus to the New World. Ponce de León made a fortune on Hispaniola (Puerto Rico). He later became governor of the island. But when he heard of an island that held the secret of eternal youth, Ponce de León was foolish enough to believe the stories.

Juan Ponce de León grew rich from his activities as a conquistador after sailing on Columbus's second voyage in 1493.

DID YOU KNOW?

The Gulf Stream is a warm current in the Atlantic Ocean. It helped the Spanish sail quickly from America back to Europe.

The humid swamps of Florida were a tough environment for Ponce de León and the Spaniards who followed him. Many contracted fever and died.

In 1513, Ponce de León left Puerto Rico with three ships and sailed through the Bahamas. When he found land, he thought he had found the famous island. It was Easter Sunday, or *Pascua de Florida* in Spanish. Leon named the new land Florida.

A New World

Florida was not an island, however. It was a peninsula of North America. Ponce de León was the first Spaniard to set foot on the mainland of the continent. Before he realized his mistake, Ponce de León sailed off to the Spanish settlement in Cuba. Seven years later, he returned to Florida. He intended to found a settlement on the "island," but was killed by native people.

DANGEROUS LAND

Ponce de León returned to Florida in 1521 with 200 men, 50 horses, and farming equipment. He dreamed of starting a new community. But the local Calusa people attacked his expedition. Ponce de León was hit in the thigh by a poison arrow. He and his men sailed for Cuba. But he was fatally injured and died soon afterward.

1528

PÁNFILO DE NARVÁEZ

Narváez and his men reach the Gulf of Mexico after their expedition in Florida—but their troubles were not at an end.

Pánfilo de Narváez was a veteran soldier of Spain's conquests in the Americas. He had a frightening appearance, with one eye and a big red beard. In 1528, he set out to look for gold in Florida. His expedition landed in Tampa Bay after being blown off course.

DID YOU KNOW?

Álvar Cabeza de Vaca recorded a story he had heard about the Seven Cities of Cíbola, said to be the home of great wealth.

Narváez and 300 men marched into northern Florida, where they defeated the Apalachee people. Narváez was disappointed to find no gold, however. Then the expedition was attacked by the Timucuas people, who used poison arrows. Even worse, there was no sign of the ships meant to pick Narváez up from the coast.

A Watery End

The Spaniards escaped on four rafts. When a storm blew up, Narváez and most of his men drowned. Only 86 survived and managed to make it to the coast of Texas.

AMAZING JOURNEY

The survivors of Narváez's expedition were enslaved by Native Americans in Texas. One, Álvar Cabeza de Vaca, fled. He met up with three more Spaniards and a black slave, Estebanico. With the help of friendly Native Americans, the group wandered across Texas and the Southwest. Amazingly, they ran into Spanish soldiers in northern Mexico in 1533 and were rescued.

Cabeza de Vaca and his colleagues were the first Europeans in the American West and the first to see buffalo on the Plains, which they found good to eat.

CÍBOLA

Once Spanish explorers found gold and silver in South and Central America, they were eager to find it in North America. That was why they were so ready to believe stories of Cíbola. According to an account by Álvar Cabeza de Vaca, the region's seven cities had fabulous riches. In 1539, expeditions set out to find them.

Cíbola, sometimes known by the Spaniards as "the Seven Cities of Gold," was said to lie in the rocky deserts of what is now New Mexico.

Hernando de Soto followed Narváez's route as far as Apalachee in Florida. In 1541, he reached the Mississippi River, where he died.

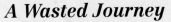

Hernando de Soto landed in Florida in 1539. He retraced Narváez's route through Florida but found nothing. His deputy, Luis de Moscoso Alvarado, explored eastern Texas and the Mexican coast. Again, he found nothing.

A Wasted Journey

The following year, Francisco de Coronado led more than 2,000 men north from Mexico. They followed the directions of Friar Niza, who said he had seen the fabled cities. All they found were villages of mud huts. Some of Coronado's men did discover the Grand Canyon—but no gold. Meanwhile, Francisco de Ulloa and Hernando de Alarcón led expeditions to the California coast. They found no sign of Cíbola.

THE LIAR FRIAR

A Franciscan monk, Friar Marcos de Niza, claimed to find Cíbola in 1539 in what is now New Mexico. His stories inspired Coronado's expedition. But Coronado's men only found villages of pueblos. The houses were built with adobe, or mud bricks dried in the sun. The villages were poor. There was no gold.

DID YOU KNOW?

De Soto introduced pigs to North America. They had escaped from his expedition. Coronado introduced the horse.

1534–1541

JACQUES CARTIER

While the Spanish explored in the South, the French explored what is now Canada. In 1534, Jacques Cartier arrived in search of a Northwest Passage to Asia. His route followed fishermen who had sailed to Newfoundland and traded with local Huron and Algonquin people.

This early map shows Europeans exploring the northeast coast of North America (north lies at the bottom of the map).

Cartier meets a group of Huron in 1535. The site of the Huron village eventually became the French colonial city of Montreal.

DID YOU KNOW?

Cartier set out to find the Northwest Passage, a route around the top of America to Asia and the Spice Islands.

Cartier did not go far inland before he headed home. But when he returned to Canada in 1535, he sailed 150 miles (240 km) up the St. Lawrence River. He discovered the site of modern-day Montreal. He thought the river might lead to the Pacific, but the way was blocked by huge rapids.

Too Cold

Cartier made a third trip to Canada in 1541. This time a French aristocrat wanted Cartier to help him start a French colony. Cartier refused. He complained that the winters were too cold and returned to France. The colonists followed a year later, by which time many had died from cold.

NEW FRANCE

Cartier's expeditions allowed France to claim territory in the Northeast of North America. The region became known as New France. The French wanted to repeat the success of the Spanish colonies in the South. The two powers clashed in Florida. French explorers set up a settlement, Fort Caroline, in 1564. The Spanish attacked and killed them all, claiming Florida for Spain.

1603–1632

SAMUEL DE CHAMPLAIN

Champlain studied the journeys of explorers such as Jacques Cartier before he traveled to Canada in 1603. He did much to encourage French settlement, including founding a colony on the island of Saint Croix. Champlain became known as the "father of New France."

Champlain founded a colony on the island of Saint Croix, near the mouth of the Saint Croix River.

DID YOU KNOW?
Champlain made the first accurate map of the East Coast as far south as what is now Rhode Island.

Champlain's expeditions led him as far south as Long Island. He also traveled inland into Canada. In 1608, Champlain led 32 colonists to settle Quebec City. The winter was so cold only nine survived.

Many Expeditions

Over the next 20 years, Champlain led different expeditions into what he called "New France." He discovered and named Lake Champlain and traveled further up the St. Lawrence River than Cartier had gone.

Champlain also explored the eastern region of the Great Lakes. The English captured him in a raid on Fort Quebec in 1629 and held him prisoner until 1632. Once freed, he became governor of Quebec City.

VOYAGEURS

Champlain inspired many French voyageurs, or travelers, to head west across America. Those who took Champlain's advice included Étienne Brulé, who traveled as far as Lake Erie and was probably the first European to see Niagara Falls. Another notable voyageur was Jean Nicollet, who got as far as Lake Michigan in 1634.

Champlain brought French monks to try to convert native peoples to Christianity. Many of these missionaries were killed by the people they met.

19

1673

JOLLIET AND MARQUETTE

Jacques Marquette consults native people about the route of the expedition. He used his knowledge of native languages to act as an interpreter.

Jacques Marquette was a French priest and Louis Jolliet a French fur trader. They both worked in the area near the Great Lakes. In 1672, the governor of New France sent them to search for a huge river he thought might flow into the Pacific: the Mississippi.

Starting from the western shore of Lake Michigan, the two men headed south along the Fox River. They sailed through Lake Winnebago and then into the Wisconsin River. That led them to the upper part of the mighty Mississippi.

Toward the Gulf of Mexico

The two men sailed down the river as far as the Arkansas River. There local people warned them of hostile tribes further south. The explorers turned back. By then Jolliet had realized that the ever-widening river did not flow into the Pacific Ocean after all but into the Gulf of Mexico.

DID YOU KNOW?

Priests were vital to exploration. They worked with local tribes and learned vital information about local geography.

MISSISSIPPI RIVER

For hundreds of years, the Mississippi River was the dividing line between America and the West. Learning what lay beyond the 2,320-mile (3,733 km) river was the ambition of every explorer. The French exploration of the river led them to claim a vast territory in what is now the southern United States. They called it Louisiana. The river marked the territory's eastern boundary.

Jolliet and Marquette and their companions study a native home as they canoe past on one of the tributaries of the Mississippi.

1682

LA SALLE

René-Robert Cavelier, Sieur de la Salle, was a French fur trader. He had traveled widely in the Great Lakes region. In 1682, he set out on an expedition to retrace Jolliet's route down the Mississippi River. This time, La Salle intended to get all the way to the river's mouth.

In 1672, the French authorities asked La Salle to explore the Mississippi, but he was too busy working as a fur trader.

DID YOU KNOW?

Ten years after he was first asked, La Salle was the first European to travel the length of the Mississippi River, in 1682.

The swamps of the American South were full of insects, dangerous animals, and disease; they were a real challenge for European settlers.

La Salle made his way down the river. He reached the Mississippi Delta on the Gulf of Mexico in April 1682. He claimed the whole area of the vast river valley for France. He named the territory Louisiana, in honor of King Louis XIV of France.

A Second Expedition

La Salle sailed from France in 1684 intending to start a colony at the mouth of the Mississippi. The voyage was a disaster; La Salle could not find the river. He set up a colony 500 miles (800 km) to the west, at Fort St. Louis. On an expedition to try to find the Mississippi again in 1687, La Salle was killed by mutineers.

La Salle claimed a huge area of North America for France, but the French rulers did little to develop it into a colony.

LOUISIANA

The area that La Salle claimed for the French crown covered the heart of the American continent. It stretched from the Great Lakes to the Gulf of Mexico and from the Appalachians to the Rocky Mountains. In 1803, the French sold the land to the United States for $11.5 million. The modern state of Louisiana occupies a fraction of the area France once owned.

23

1497–1508

JOHN AND SEBASTIAN CABOT

John Cabot was a merchant from Venice who settled in the English port of Bristol. Cabot sailed for North America in May 1497. He believed that there must be a short route to Asia around the top of the American continent. His voyage was the first recorded attempt to find the Northwest Passage.

This replica of John Cabot's ship Matthew *was built in Bristol in 1997. The original ship would have had a crew of about 18 sailors, possibly including Cabot's teenage son, Sebastian.*

DID YOU KNOW?

John Cabot made his first voyage on behalf of King Henry VII of England. But Cabot paid for the voyage himself.

This engraving shows John and Sebastian Cabot landing in Newfoundland in 1497. No one knows if such a landing actually took place.

DISCOVERY OF NORTH AMERICA, BY JOHN AND SEBASTIAN CABOT

Accompanied by his son, Sebastian, Cabot explored Nova Scotia and the far north of the North American coast. They did not find a passage. John Cabot set out on a second voyage in 1498, this time without his son. John Cabot was never heard from again.

Sebastian Sets Sail

Whatever had happened to his father, Sebastian Cabot did not give up. In 1508, he claimed to have crossed the Atlantic again. He said he sailed up the coast of Labrador before the freezing cold stopped him going any further. Some people think he never actually made the voyages. In any case, he did not find the passage he was looking for.

NORTHWEST PASSAGE

Like the Cabots, many people believed it must to possible to sail north of the Americas to Asia. That would open new trade routes to China and the Spice Islands. A series of Portuguese, French, Spanish, and English explorers tried to find the elusive route in the 16th century. No one succeeded.

1576–1578

MARTIN FROBISHER

PICTVRA VEL DELINEATIO HOMINVM NVPER EX ANGLIA AD-
vectorum, una cum eorum armis, tentoriis, & naviculis

This drawing of Inuit using kayaks for hunting seabirds comes from an early account of Frobisher's travels.

In 1576, a group of London merchants hired the sailor Martin Frobisher to find the Northwest Passage. Frobisher and his three ships passed the southern tip of Greenland and sailed on west. He found what he thought was a strait leading west; today we know it is a bay, called Frobisher Bay.

Frobisher met local Inuit people. An Inuit agreed to lead Frobisher up the strait. Instead, the Inuit kidnapped five of Frobisher's crew. Frobisher abandoned his expedition and sailed back to England. He brought back many rocks that glittered with what looked like gold.

Return to Frobisher Bay

In London, Frobisher's backers wanted more of the "gold." Frobisher made a second expedition in 1577 to rescue his shipmates. He did not find his men, but brought back more rocks. His third expedition in 1578 aimed to set up a colony on Baffin Island. But the conditions were too cold. The colonists made Frobisher take them home.

The tons of iron pyrites that Frobisher took back to London were worthless—but his backers were greedy for more "gold."

FOOL'S GOLD

Frobisher's backers tried for five years to smelt gold or silver from the 1,350 tons (1,225 t) of rock he had brought back. It turned out to be worthless. Their company went bust, for which they blamed Frobisher. The rock turned out to be iron pyrites. It resembles an ore containing precious metals but is actually worthless. That is why it is commonly known as "fool's gold."

On Baffin Island, Frobisher sailed up what he believed was a long strait. It was actually a large inlet, today named Frobisher Bay.

DID YOU KNOW?

On his second expedition, Frobisher captured an Inuit man, woman, and child and took them back to England.

1607–1611

HENRY HUDSON

After a century of exploration, the Northwest Passage had not been found. Ice had forced back explorers who sailed too far north, such as the Englishman John Davis. In 1607, the Muscovy Company hired the English sailor Henry Hudson to find a sea route to Asia via the west.

Native Americans watch as Henry Hudson's ship Half Moon *sails into New York Harbor in 1609.*

DID YOU KNOW?

European countries were competitive about exploration. The English banned Hudson from working for the Dutch.

Hudson led two expeditions to find the passage, in 1607 and 1608. Both times, icebergs blocked his way. On his third expedition, Hudson sailed on behalf of the Dutch East India Company.

The Hudson River

In spring 1609, ice again forced Hudson to abandon his voyage north. He sailed south and into what is now New York Harbor. He sailed up the tidal river that is now named for him. The salty water made him hope this was the sea passage he was looking for. When he realized that it was a river, he gave up. He stopped at Albany, New York.

Hudson sailed up the river that now bears his name as far as the site of modern-day Albany, New York.

UNUSABLE ROUTE

John Cabot made the first attempt to find the Northwest Passage in 1497. It was not until over 400 years later that the Norwegian Roald Amundsen successfully sailed through it in 1903. But the route was not the short-cut to Asia that early geographers had hoped for. It lay inside the Arctic Circle, where the sea was frozen for most of the year.

1607–1611

Another Expedition

Hudson sailed again for North America in 1610 on the *Discovery*. This time, his expedition had English backers. On June 24, 1610, Hudson sailed through the "Hudson Strait" and found a huge body of water opening up before him.

A Huge Bay

Hudson named the body of water the Bay of God's Mercies. It is now named for him: Hudson Bay. He sailed down its east coast, where he hoped to find a route to the west that was free of ice. He reached James Bay before he realized there was no way out.

By the time Hudson realized Hudson Bay had no outlet to the Pacific, it was too late to escape before the water froze and trapped the ship for the winter.

DID YOU KNOW?

Hudson's backers spent another 20 years sending explorers to look for the Northwest Passage. None succeeded.

Natives row out to meet Hudson's ship Half Moon. *Hudson was sailing on behalf of the Dutch; the ship's original name was* Halve Maen.

Miserable Winter

Hudson's error proved fatal. He could not get out of the bay before the ship was trapped by the ice. He was forced to spend the winter there. The crew was so miserable it mutinied. Once the ice had melted enough for *Discovery* to sail, the sailors cast Hudson adrift.

CAST ADRIFT

In June 1611, the rebellious crew of the Discovery *forced Hudson, his young son, and some sick crewmen to leave the ship. They were put into a small boat with a gun, ammunition, and some rations. The boat was cast adrift. The men's chances of survival were zero, and they were never heard of again. The mutineers later said that Hudson had kept all the rations for himself.*

Hudson and his companions, including his son John, had no chance of survival after they were cast adrift.

1607–1609

JOHN SMITH

John Smith was a soldier in Europe before he helped found the first permanent English settlement in America, Jamestown, Virginia, in 1607. Smith and Christopher Newport were commissioned to take 120 colonists to North America. Smith's writings about Virginia encouraged English settlement there.

Pocahontas gets in the way as her father, chief of the Powhatan, prepares to kill John Smith. According to a story told many years later by Smith, the teenage girl saved his life.

John Smith intended his descriptions of Virginia to attract more English settlers to the colony, so he stressed the best things about it.

The expedition sailed up the James River and founded Jamestown. From there, Smith made expeditions inland and to Chesapeake Bay and the New England coast. He wrote in great detail about the plants and animals he saw. He said the colonists did not make enough use of the natural resources.

Captured

On one trip, Smith was taken prisoner by the Powhatan people. According to a story Smith told long afterward, he was sentenced to death but was spared by the intervention of the chief's daughter, Pocahontas. Smith returned to England in 1609. He did not return to North America and died in 1631.

DID YOU KNOW?

Smith's colleague Christopher Newport had crossed the Atlantic previously with the English seafarer Sir Francis Drake.

POCAHONTAS

Late in his life, John Smith told a story about how Pocahontas saved his life in 1608. Her father, the chief of the Powhatan, was about to kill Smith when the 13-year-old girl stopped him. Five years later, Pocahontas was captured by the English. She became a Christian and took the name Rebecca. With her English husband, John Rolfe, she traveled to London in 1616. She was the talk of the town. She died on the voyage home.

1773

DANIEL BOONE

Daniel Boone fights off a Cherokee who has just killed his young son, James, in the Cumberland Gap in 1773.

Daniel Boone was the most famous of the men who explored the interior of the United States inland from the settled coast. Boone was a crack shot. He spent months in the wilderness hunting, using skills he learned from Native Americans. He and his colleagues are known as frontiersmen.

Boone was determined to find a way through the Appalachian Mountains to Kentucky. The route lay through thick forests full of hostile Native Americans. In 1773, Boone's eldest son, James, was killed by Cherokees.

Westward Bound

Boone finally crossed the mountains through the Cumberland Gap. His team of loggers built the Wilderness Road. It was a vital route for settlers heading west. Boone himself later became famous for telling tall stories about his adventures on the frontier.

CUMBERLAND GAP

The Cumberland Gap is a natural pass through the Appalachian Mountains that separate the East Coast from the rest of North America. Named for an English general, the Duke of Cumberland, the pass was first discovered in 1750 by Thomas Walker. Native Americans had long used the pass, but Boone widened it. The Wilderness Road he built gave settlers an easy route over the mountains from the 1770s.

The Cumberland Gap was a natural pass through the Appalachian Mountains to Kentucky and the western plains.

1804–1806

LEWIS AND CLARK

In 1803, the United States acquired vast new territories in the West. The following year, President Thomas Jefferson asked Meriwether Lewis and William Clark to make the first journey across America to the Pacific Ocean. They were tasked to explore the new territory.

The Corps of Discovery sailed down the Clearwater River in Idaho in October 1805. It led them to the Snake River.

William Clark's family had moved to Kentucky, where Clark made a name for himself as a rugged frontiersman.

Lewis was a soldier who had studied natural sciences. Clark was also a soldier and a frontiersman. They would find out what plants and animals were in the new territory and how they could be exploited.

Corps of Discovery

Clark handpicked the Corps of Discovery. A total of 33 people set out along the Missouri River. Some of the travelers were French fur trappers, who knew the upper Mississippi region well. Lewis and Clark met Toussaint Charbonneau, a French trapper, and his wife, Sacajawea. The Shoshone woman was about to have a baby, but she still joined the expedition.

LOUISIANA PURCHASE

In 1803, the United States bought the French territory of Louisiana. The Louisiana Purchase covered 828,000 square miles (2 million sq km) west of the Mississippi River. It doubled the size of the United States, expanding it to the Rocky Mountains. The area included all or part of what are now 15 U.S. states. The purchase was a great spur to exploration in the West.

Invaluable Help

Sacajawea's knowledge of the area to the west was vital to the success of the expedition. She had made the journey through the Rocky Mountains to the Pacific Ocean with the Shoshone on their annual buffalo hunt.

Having crossed the Great Plains, as Clark named them, the expedition struggled across the Rockies. They encountered grizzly bears and rattlesnakes. But with Sacajawea's advice, they found the way through the mountains.

Sacajawea was not the only source of help. Some of the native peoples the explorers met showed them the way. Others, however, were hostile.

These illustrations show episodes from the expedition: talking to Native Americans (top), capsizing (center), and shooting bears (bottom).

DID YOU KNOW?

When the Corps reached the Clearwater Valley, the Nez Percés drew them maps of how to reach the Pacific.

The Ocean

Sacajawea convinced the Shoshone to help Lewis and Clark reach the Pacific. When the Shoshone gave him salmon to eat, Clark realized the ocean must be close. The Corps reached the Columbia River, where they rode the rapids through the Cascade Mountains and reached the Pacific on November 20, 1805. The Corps stayed the winter there before turning for home. They reached St. Louis in September the next year. Their journey had taken two years and ten months.

SACAJAWEA

Without Sacajawea's knowledge of the land and Native American tribes, the expedition would have failed. On the journey, the young woman gave birth to a baby boy, whom Clark nicknamed "Pomp." When the party finally crossed the Great Divide of the Rockies, Sacajawea was reunited with her family. She had not seen them for five years, since she was captured by the tribes who sold her to Charbonneau.

The Columbia River was the final part of the journey. Its rapids took the Corps of Discovery from the Rocky Mountains to the Pacific Coast.

1823–1830

JEDEDIAH SMITH

This 19th-century painting shows two mountain men fishing in a creek. Mountain men could survive for months in the wilderness.

After the Louisiana Purchase in 1803 opened the West to exploration, a new breed of pioneers emerged: the mountain men. Jedediah Smith was one of the most famous. He explored the Rocky Mountains between 1823 and 1825 with the Ashley Company. In 1826, he and two companions decided to head further west in order to hunt for beaver.

DID YOU KNOW?

With the help of the Crow people, Smith discovered South Pass, the fastest route from the Rocky Mountains to California.

Smith's party traveled through Utah and across the Colorado River to northern Arizona. They found no beaver. Instead, they were astonished to discover a forbidding landscape of semidesert. They nearly died of heat and exhaustion, but were saved by the local Mojave.

Into California

The Mojave told Smith about California to the west. They said it was cattle country. Smith immediately set out, despite the fact that California was in Spanish Mexico, not the United States. The mountain men crossed the Mojave Desert and arrived close to present-day Los Angeles. They had made the first overland expedition to California.

WILLIAM H. ASHLEY

William Ashley was a fur trader who settled in Missouri. He hired a group of fur trappers, but he also went with them to explore the country. Many of Ashley's recruits became famous mountain men, like Jim Bridger and Jedediah Smith. Such men blazed trails through the Midwest and the Rocky Mountains. They had to battle both harsh conditions and hostile native peoples.

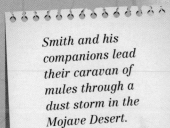

Smith and his companions lead their caravan of mules through a dust storm in the Mojave Desert.

California

In California, Smith asked the Mexican governor for supplies and free passage through the territory. Instead, the governor put Smith under arrest. He freed him when Smith agreed to return home and never set foot in California again—an agreement Smith immediately broke.

A religious man, Smith thought he was in the right and took no notice of the authorities. He stayed in California, spending the winter in the mountains of the San Joaquin valley.

Mountain men explored Bear River in Utah in 1843. The river valley was on the route of the California and Oregon wagon trails.

The desert landscape of scrub and Joshua trees created a difficult ordeal for Smith and his men on their way back east from California.

WAGON TRANS

As the mountain men opened trails, wagons became a familiar sight on the Great Plains. Settlers headed west to seek land to farm. They traveled in groups for protection. They gathered in Independence, Missouri, before taking the Santa Fe Trail or other trails. The journey to California could take six months. Most settlers walked the whole way: the wagons carried supplies or those too weak to walk.

Disastrous Trip

The journey back east was a nightmare. The Mojave had changed their minds about helping Smith. They attacked the party and killed 10 men. The survivors returned to California, where Smith was jailed but later released. He headed east, but was ambushed again, Smith lost another 10 men. He finally ran out of luck on an expedition in Kansas in 1830, when he was killed by Comanches.

DID YOU KNOW?

A grizzly bear attacked Smith in 1824. It tore his scalp and ear but Smith got his friend to stitch his face back together.

1789–1793

ALEXANDER MACKENZIE

Alexander Mackenzie was a Scot who became a fur trapper in Canada. Mackenzie was convinced there was a water route to the Pacific Ocean. As he hunted for it, he made the first crossing of North America. He reached the Pacific in 1793, 10 years before Lewis and Clark.

Mackenzie moved to North America from Scotland in 1774. His family sent him to Canada to escape the American Revolutionary War.

DID YOU KNOW?

Although Mackenzie rushed back east with news of his route to the Pacific, no one thought it had any commercial use.

Explorers camp near Great Slave Lake in Canada. Mackenzie reached the lake in 1789 before heading along what is now Mackenzie River.

On Mackenzie's first expedition in 1789, he sailed up Slave River. He then traveled for 40 days up another river, now called the Mackenzie. But the river brought him to the edge of the Arctic Ocean, not the Pacific as he had hoped.

Second Expedition

For Mackenzie's second expedition in 1793, he took a 25-foot (8 m) long canoe and a nine-man team. High in the Rockies, the canoe was wrecked, and the expedition had to continue on foot. They eventually met the Bella Coola people, who gave them new canoes. After nine months, Mackenzie finally made it to the Pacific Ocean.

CANADIAN INTERIOR

The interior of Canada contains some of the most difficult and inhospitable terrain for an explorer. The distances are huge. Mountains and countless lakes and rivers bar the way. There are fewer native peoples than in the United States. In addition, any explorer had to deal with long, freezing winters, ice, mosquitoes, and scarce supplies of food other than fish.

GLOSSARY

adobe A building material made from bricks of dried mud.

colony A settlement founded in a new territory by people from another country.

continent A very large landmass.

corps A group of people who act together and are instructed by the same leaders.

expedition A journey made for a particular purpose.

fort A well-defended building or settlement.

governor An official who governs a colony on behalf of the original country of the settlers.

mutiny A revolt by soldiers or sailors against their senior officers.

Northwest Passage A route to Asia around the north of the American continent; many Europeans believed such a route must exist.

ore A mineral from which a precious or useful metal can be extracted.

pass A gap in a mountain range that provides a route for travelers.

pueblo A Native American village in the Southwest built of flat-roofed houses, also called pueblos.

rapids A part of a river where the current runs quickly over many rocks.

rations A limited supply of food.

strait A narrow sea passage that connects two larger bodies of water.

trapper Someone who traps animals for their fur.

tributary A smaller river that runs into a bigger one.

wilderness An unsettled region where nobody lives.

FURTHER INFORMATION

Books

Cox, Caroline, and Ken Albala. *Opening Up North America: 1497–1800* (Discovery and Exploration). Chelsea House Publications, 2010.

Feinstein, Stephen. *Columbus: Opening Up the New World* (Great Explorers of the World). Enslow Publishers, 2009.

Greenway, Shirley. *Exploration of North America* (History of Exploration). Newforest Press, 2010.

Hernandez, Roger E. *Early Explorations: The 1500s* (Hispanic Americans). Marshall Cavendish Children's Books, 2008.

Isserman, Maurice. *Exploring North America: 1800–1900* (Discovery and Exploration). Chelsea House Publications, 2010.

Taylor-Butler, Christine. *Explorers of North America: Lewis and Clark* (True Books: American History). Childrens Press, 2007.

Websites

http://www.history.com/topics/exploration-of-North-America
History.com guide to the history of American exploration.

www.americanjourneys.org
A highlights timeline with 18,000 pages of eyewitness accounts from the history of exploration in America.

INDEX